D1629510

Dedicated to with Special Thanks

Steven Roth

**For providing me with the facility
in which I found this wisdom.**

**If the Horse is dead.....
Get off.....**

A bad workman,
is accustomed to quarreling
with his tools.

**The miser starves himself,
so his heirs may feast.**

**He who knows himself best,
esteems himself least.**

The excesses of youth
are drafts upon old age,
payable with interest.

Remembering an injury often hurts more than receiving it.

We all have two education's
one we receive from others
and one we give ourselves.

**Never marry without Love,
or Love without reason.**

**Many come to bring
their clothes to church,
rather than themselves.**

We often need to repent
for saying too much,
seldom for saying too little.

**He who says what he thinks,
must also hear what he
does not think.**

**Be cautious of believing ill,
but more cautious
of repeating it.**

**Reading enriches the mind,
conversation polishes it.**

**The wise man
 knows the fool,
 but the fool,
 knows not the wise man.**

**Your mirror,
will tell you what
none of your friends will.**

**Pride hides our faults,
and magnifies the faults
of others.**

**He that has
good health,
is young.**

**He is rich,
who owes nothing.**

Compliments cost nothing.

It is good to know the failings
of our friends,
but not to publish them.

A man may talk
like a wise man,
but act like a fool.

**Experience and wisdom
are two great fortune-tellers.**

It is better to have wisdom
without learning,
than learning without
wisdom.

**Philosophy is to poetry
what old age is to youth......
facts against fiction.**

Cheerfulness should be
encouraged in youth,
or it cannot be expected
in old age.

The whole world is turned

Upside down

every twenty-four hours.

**We should forgive freely,
even if we don't forget.**

**The minds of men differ
as much as their faces.**

shadows

shadows

**Like our
our wishes lengthen
as our shine declines.**

Ambition is like love,
impatient of delays
and rivals.

**Night shows stars
and women in
a better light.**

Love, like a cold bath,
seldom leaves us as it found us.

I love my enemies,
for it is from them
I learn my faults.

**If you think twice
before you speak,
you will speak twice
the better for it.**

Revenge,
thought at first sweet,
becomes bitter
as it comes back at you.

Avoid if possible, spending money before you have it.

**Avoid buying
what you do not want,
even if it is on sale.**

**The troubles we imagine,
are often worse
than the real ones.**

**If you desire
to be wiser,
think yourself
not wise enough.**

**It is important
to gather knowledge,
more important
to use it.**

A wise man
endeavors to shine
in himself.......
A fool tries to
outshine others.

He that talks of all he knows, is likely to talk more than he knows.

There are a great
many asses
without long ears.

Anyone who has good health is rich, it is unfortunate that they don't know it until it is gone.

A false friend and
a shadow attend us
only when the sun
shines.

Three words of advice......

Don't give any.

**Don't talk too fast,
you might have to eat
your words.**

No one can help everyone, but everyone can help someone.

Never argue with a
woman when she is
tired or rested.

Time does heal all wounds, you just have to give them air and stop 'picking' at them.

One good head is better than a great many hands.

Rich men,
depend on the poor,
as well as the poor on them.

Friendship, like health,
is not duly prized
until it is lost.

Those who forgive
most shall be
most forgiven.

Power will intoxicate the best hearts, as wine overpowers the strongest heads.

**Finding love is easy,
keeping it takes time
and effort.**

If you are healthy,
don't be smug about it......
we all unravel in time.

Faith is what lets you understand why you don't always get what you pray for.

Women never really understand why men don't get excited about dust.

Most education occurs after you leave school.

Politics is the art of calling:
  Spending ~ Investments
  Swamps ~ Wetlands
  Dumps ~ Landfills

**To conserve energy,
start s l o w l y ~~~
then taper off.**

There were times
when I thought that
I didn't need love,
but that was when
I was working too hard.

**Love is something
I've always had,
because my parents
gave it to me.**

Health is certainly
something you crave
for as you get older.

**Along the way,
you learn that happiness
is more than a puppy,
but less than money.**

When you pray, **you** have to
be willing to accept the answer,
even if it isn't the one **you**
thought was right.

**To hold on to your man
remember..........
the little boy inside.**

Never guess the
size of a woman,
it always creates
big problems.

Praise your Children
as you appraise them.

Just because you
like your work~~~
it doesn't mean that
it isn't taxing~~~

Honey & Money both very sticky and both very sweet.

**If anyone tries to tell
you that armchair travel
is the best way to travel~~~
ask them where they
have been?**

**Go ahead
plan for tomorrow,
but don't
bank on it.**

In the beginning...
I wondered where
It would all end....
Lucky for me.....
I still do.

Any **ending**
you are around for
is a good **ending.**

Life is a laughing matter.

Happiness
comes from many places,
but the best place to
find it is in you.

Money is never
what makes you
really rich.

Love is sometimes
hardest to see when it
is right in front of you.

Happiness does not depend upon conditions **outside** of us, but upon conditions **inside** of us.

Always be guided by God's will instead of your own will.

**Go ahead....
Get mad.....
But get over it!**

If you have credit,
remember to
give credit.

**Be careful what
you ask for~~~~
you might get it.**

**Money is a good servant,
but a hard master.**

IF you stew about
tomorrow
you are certain to
cook up trouble.

Yesterday is gone.
Remember that.

May you live as long as you want, and may you want as long as you live.

Today is "the good old days";
all that is missing is the soft
patina of nostaliga.

Laughter is music, in its finest form.

**Good Health~~~~~
It can not be bought
but it can be earned.**

**Prayer:
It puts us "on-line"
with God.**

Simply:
Love is a blessing.

**Health:
The gift money can't
buy.**

Health is a good habit.... Don't break it.

If the best things in life are free, why is the next best so expensive?

Be sure to keep love with you, you never know when someone may need it.

Prayer needs to be your first resort, not your last.

If love makes the world
go around,
it is happiness that keeps
it turning.

Love...like chocolate
can be......
sweet, hard and sticky.

It is amazing
how much more it hurts
to fall when someone
sees you do it.

**Young people
are works of nature,
and the old, are works
of art.**

**Men, are never too busy
to talk about how busy
they are.**

When you are young,
you wish to change the
world.
When you are old,
you wish to change the
young.

No matter how "cool"
you look in your high-
school yearbook~~~
in twenty years,
your kids will laugh.

It is good to remember,
work with the construction
crew, not the wrecking crew.

Everything comes to those who wait~~~~

as long as they work while they wait.

A poor man is not the man without money, but the man without a dream.

It took about 75 years for movies to go from silent to unspeakable.

**If you fill your life with
regrets of yesterday,
and fears of tomorrow,
you will have no time to
be thankful for today.**

Don't live your life in the "past" lane.

I'm not afraid of dying,
I just don't want to be
there when it happens.

In matters that are controversial, I always see both points of view, the wrong one and mine.

Money can't buy happiness,
but it can help us
be miserable in style.

The 1st duty of Love is to listen.

**Only love can be divided
endlessly and still not
diminish.**

What we prevent needs no cure.

There is no tranquilizer
more effective than a few
kind words and deeds.

Most people are about
as happy as they make
up their minds to be.

**More men fail
through lack of purpose
than lack of talent.**

If you think education is expensive, observe the greater cost of ignorance.

You are better off
not knowing how
sausages and laws
are made.

When I was a child,
people quit spending
when they ran out of
money.

The surest way to get
somewhere is to know
where you are going.

We travel faster now,
but I don't know if
we go to better things.

**You cannot be optimistic
when you look through
misty optics.**

The best way to prepare for tomorrow is to take care of today.

Take time to think where
you are going,
or you might not like
where you end up.

Try to make at least one person laugh today.

Anyone who tells you it's
better to have loved and lost
than to have never loved at all,
has never really loved or lost.

Prayer can change things~~~
You

You don't have to be wise to be educated.

We have the best politicians money can buy.

Always remember.....
your character stays
in the room long after
you leave.

Our children are the roots of tomorrow.

**You can give without
loving ~~~~~~
but you can't love
without giving.**

True love
never truly fails.

Love that is true does nothing false.

**We do not find
happiness,
it finds us.**

Happiness is not in getting
what you want;
it is being content with
what you have.

**The heart of education,
is the education
of the heart.**

**The measure of a man
is not in how tall he is,
but in how much he is
looked up to.**

The great aim of education is knowledge followed by action.

Without work.....
 I get bored...
 I develop vices...
 and have to go back
 to work to pay for them.

Talking
seldom does the
job.

**Life is full of angles
but success comes from
the try-angle.**

Exaggeration ~~~~~~

weakens

**Knowledge
can be taught~~~~~~
Wisdom
must be earned~~~**

Keep your eye on the goal,

**that way the
obstacles
can't block your view.**

Fanning a fire can cause
more flame,
more smoke,
more warmth,
but for a shorter time.

Beginnings are always easiest to see from the end.

Up
hill is always harder,
when you are thinking d
o
w
n
h
i
l
l.

Look at road construction, and note how rough things always get before they get smooth.

**Work does interfere
with pleasure~~~~
but it is work that
makes pleasure possible.**

You can not pass your love on to anyone who is not open to receive.

**When you fall in love,
keep it in mind
that most times you fall
it hurts.**

**With Love~~~~~~~~
understanding
comes naturally.**

**Children like apples,
when polished
are more appealing.**

If you can't see the problem, you certainly won't find a solution.

**Success takes a backbone,
not a wishbone.**

Doesn't it seem like
cheap chocolate should
have fewer calories?

When I travel I seldom take
pictures~~~~~
I take movies with my mind
and run them over and over.

Indecision~~~~~~
Is the key to flexibility.

You can't tell which way
the train went by looking
at the track.

**There is absolutely
no substitute for a
genuine lack of preperation.**

Sometimes too much
to drink is not enough.

The facts, although
interesting,
are irrelevant.

Someone who thinks
logically is a nice contrast
to the real world.

**Friends may come and go,
but enemies accumulate.**

If you think that there is good in everybody, you have not met everybody.

If you can smile when
things go wrong,
you have someone in mind
to blame it on.

One seventh of your life is spent on Monday.

Never wrestle with a pig~~~~
you both get dirty,
and the pig likes it.

The trouble with life is,
you are halfway through
before you realize that it
is a "do it yourself" thing.

Even a dog can shake hands.

Not one shred of evidence supports the notion that life is serious.

**The more you run over
a dead cat~~~~~~~
the flatter it gets.**

**Happiness,
comes from within
and without.**

**Laughing at yourself
is always acceptable.**

Travel is the key to broadening your education and your understanding of it.

If you can't fight~~~~~
and you can't flee,
flow~~~~~~~~~

Coping:

   Rule#1:
   Don't sweat the small stuff.
   Rule#2:
   It is all small stuff.

Marriage is the only war in which we sleep with the enemy.

**To get back on your feet,
miss two car payments.**

**Flies cause disease~~~~~
keep yours zipped.**

**Never play leap frog
with a unicorn.**

**Remember that a kick
in the ass is a step forward.**

He who hesitates is not only
lost, but miles from the next exit.

**Time is natures way
of keeping everything
from happening at once.**

Don't speak ill of your enemies,
ignoring them is better.

**Don't speak of
your talents,
let them speak
for you.**

**Don't acquire the eating habit.
Eat to live, not live to eat.**

**Don't fail to give time
to thought~~~~~~~
it pays excellent
dividends.**

A simple Rule:
Don't go, when "to go or not
to go" becomes a struggle.

Nothing expands the mind as far as travel.

**Don't be too anxious
to get in the swim~~~~~~
Many have drown there.**

**Don't open your heart
to love, until it proves
its idenity.**

Keep in mind that life's stepping stones are often very slippery~~~~watch your step.

**Don't dream of happiness~~~
Deserve it.**

**Don't be afraid to fail,
be however too proud
to cease trying.**

**Don't spend time wondering
if you are in love with someone,
you obviously are not or you
would know.**

The longer you keep
your temper the more
it will improve.

Life is like a ladder~~~

Every step is either   up   or

d

o

w

n.

It is hard to keep your shirt on when you are getting something off your chest.

A true test of character is being put on a pedestal and not looking down on those who put you there.

**Silence is not golden,
it is safe.**

**The Ten Commandments
are not multiple choice.**

The only sharp-edged tool that gets sharper with use is the tongue.

If everything is coming your way, you are in the wrong lane.

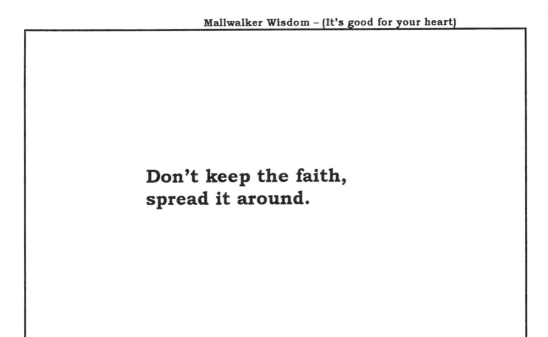

**Don't keep the faith,
spread it around.**

Nobody has ever come up with a substitute for friendship.

**The way to be happy ever-after~~~~
is not to be after too much.**

Promises may get friends, but it is performance that keeps them.

**Too many people miss
the silver lining because
they are expecting gold.**

**Hardening of the heart,
is worse than hardening
of the arteries.**

**Man's limitations are not
what he can not do~~~~~
but what he ought to do
and does not.**

If your husband tells you
that the lipstick on his shirt
is Tomato Juice~~~~~~~~
Find the Tomato!

**Know-how is especially
valuable to someone who
does not know how.**

Teenagers get confused
when advised:
      "Find Yourself"
by some, and
      "Get Lost"
by others.

**To have failed is bad~~~~~~~
to be content with it is
much worse.**

**Politicians are very good
at answering questions
that no one asked.**

**Worse than a quitter
is someone afraid to
begin.**

Old age is always
about fifteen years
from now.

When the prices
on the menu don't
matter to you,
calories no doubt will.

If you want rainbows~~~~
Ya gotta have rain.

Happiness is a choice~~~~~
YOURS!

A bachelor has a list of near Mrs.

I think sometimes that
I have learned more than
I understand.

If your day is hemmed with prayer, it is less likely to unravel.

When some people speak
of their family tree,
they trim a branch or two.

Perhaps you are a "Mallwalker" with
additional wisdom that you would like to
share, if so please jot it down and send it
to me. If another volume of "Mallwalker Wisdom"
is published, you could be part of it. Thank you.

**Nancy H Phillips
707 State Route 12
Greene, New York 13778**